From my Kitchen Window

And Other Places

Pat Lomax

British Library Cataloguing in Publication Data:

a catalogue record for this publication is available from the British Library

ISBN   978-1-912052-65-3

Unless otherwise stated, Bible verses are from the NIV (New International Version) used by permission of the International Bible Society.

Typeset in 13.0 Baskerville at Dundee, Scotland

Contents

Acknowledgements

My thanks go to Keith Petersen, who, with his writer's hat on, made helpful edits — and wearing his photographer's hat, kept me at it till I had an acceptable cover design!

I also appreciate the help of Jock Stein of Handsel Press in the publishing of this book.

Introduction

Slowly, slowly, I lift the camera. There is a flash of wings. Once again I am too late! I wait some time but coffee is getting cold. I pick up the mug and now, with my hands full, the bird alights, perfectly poised for that beautiful, but unobtainable, shot! I am in the kitchen looking out of the window, watching the constant coming and going of birds, eating and squabbling over the food that I have put out. Ideally I would have the tripod set up, but it isn't practical – and then there are two windows!

These days there is more time to 'stand and stare' as the Covid 19 coronavirus pandemic grips the world and our movements are restricted. Although we go out only for essential purposes, the birds and other creatures are free! It is fascinating to watch them. Some are assertive, some gentle, some greedy. There are messy eaters and dainty eaters; ones that go round in a crowd, others individually. All are identified by the beautiful colouring and markings of their feathers – each feather a wonder, each bird a wonder.

Suddenly, another movement. A little mouse looks nervously around, nose twitching, large ears identifying it as a field mouse (sometimes known as a wood mouse). It finds a sunflower seed and sits a moment nibbling then quickly shoots back into the safety of the wall.

I think of the wildlife in its various forms that has come my way during this past year, all pointing to a God of abundance, of beauty and order – and of LIFE! Each bird, animal, plant and insect has a part to play in the amazing environment in which man has been placed and has been given responsibility – sadly so often neglected.

March 2020

"For since the creation of the world God's invisible qualities – his eternal power and divine nature – have been clearly seen. . ." Genesis 2:6 NKJV

6

Left: Dunnock, Blackcap and Blue Tit. A watermelon makes a feeding dish for a while.

Right: Chiffchaff. This little chiffchaff would probably normally have gone un-noticed. However, a walk to the nearby field and wood was to be treasured. Taking time to enjoy and look more carefully, I saw so much more than I usually did.

Like the chiffchaff, the blackcap was no doubt a recent arrival from Europe having spent the winter in warmer climes, to the envy of some! Migration is surely one of the wonders of God's provision. Many birds, butterflies and animals are equipped with all that is essential to guide them, often thousands of miles, to where they will best survive or breed. Birds have tiny concentrations of iron in their inner ear which help them navigate by using the Earth's magnetic field. They are also guided by the sun, stars, landmarks and apparently even smell.

Pheasant flaps and calls to keep his harem in order!

I feel a bit guilty going out in the car, driving just a little way – but was pleased to catch this.

April 2020

". . . without Him nothing was made that has been made." John 1:3

Left: Goldfinch and *Above*: Male Sparrow
— both looking smart for the Spring.

I notice little field mice peeping out from around the wall.

A Magpie arrives.

11

New life unfolds and pushes up in the garden and woods. Ferns and bracken unfurl. Violets and wood sorrel show shyly; each a miracle. Can anyone pause and not marvel at the greatness of the One who brings such beautiful life and fragrance out of the earth, year after year?

Honesty

Wild Violet

Wood Sorrel

Wood Sorrel

Fern unfurling

The birds have been looking their best but now the hard work begins! The blue tits clear out the old nest material and take in new soft moss. An old photo of the robin shows he/she is beginning to look a bit ragged this time of year. Long tailed tits (above left) make a beautiful round nest with moss and lichen stitched together with spider's webs and lined with feathers, almost enclosed at the top (no photo unfortunately). Although it can take up to a month to painstakingly make, it expands so can hold up to sixteen chicks! How do they know how to do that? Many birds ornate their nests with petals if they can find them. Blue tits have been known to use lavender.

Far left: Robin and Coal Tit

May 2020

"See! The winter is past . . . the season of singing has come . . ."
Song of Songs 2:11-12

The wonderful sound of the dawn chorus sounds like a great rejoicing, but it is really a declaration of strength — of being able to hold a territory with plenty of food for a family, while also warning off any rival males who may be looking to move in.

Left: Thrush enjoying the berries on the ivy.

Above: Great Tit on the bird bath looking splendid

Above: Coal Tit in the pine tree.

Right: Male Great Spotted Woodpecker,
(identified by the red patch on back of head),
looking so smart, comes for a visit from time to
time.

Blue Tit

The blue tit and robin are still feeding nestlings while the young starlings have already fledged. Somehow the parent birds seem to know what is just right for their young, whatever stage they are at. Note the blue tit and the robin (right) with little grubs for their nestlings.

Young Starling

Young Starling already feeding itself.

June 2020

"See! The winter is past . . . Flowers appear on the earth . . ."
Song of Songs 2:11-12

Lovely to see blue cornflower by the wayside, wild iris and wild orchids on daily walks.

The roots and leaves of the wild flag iris were used in Scotland for traditional natural dye for both tartan and tweed. The roots were also made into ink and in many parts of the Highlands were also used medicinally.

Blue tit young are growing.

Blue tit and sparrow try out the bird bath.

Wild roses appear in the hedgerow.

White-tailed bumble bee, one of several kinds around, gathers pollen from the June rose.

A hedgehog visitor appears in the garden, snuffling up any bird seed that might be around. I decide to provide her own dish.

An ease in restrictions allows a welcome trip to the beach. A very persistent male sparrow suitor eventually gets seen off by the female!

Top right: Stranded Jellyfish

Right: Sea weed makes a splash of colour.

Top left: Yellowhammer waits to feed young.
Lower left: Blue Damselfly

The swallows arrive having travelled some 8,000 miles almost non-stop from South Africa, catching flies and insects as they fly, enabling them to do the journey in about six weeks. During spring and summer, flies, insects and bugs are in abundance over the farmland in UK; then it is back again to South Africa for winter, this time with their young! Somehow they know where to go!

27

July 2020

"Let everything that has breath praise the Lord. Praise the Lord." Psalm 150:6

A wonderful visit to cliffs where the sea birds come to nest year after year, jostling for their own space on the narrow shelves, often coming back to the exact same spot each year.

Anticlockwise: Razorbill, Kittiwake and Guillemot, Pink Campion, Puffin, Kittiwake with chick, Harebell, Fulmars.

29

A boat trip to the Isle of May becomes possible. Never get tired of watching the puffins. The terns, of course, had to be dodged and attacks fended off as the boat landed just where they were breeding. But no wonder they are defensive having flown around 12,00 miles to get here!

31

August 2020

"God gave Solomon wisdom and very great insight . . . He was wiser than anyone else . . . And his fame spread to all the surrounding nations . . . He also spoke about animals and birds . . . From all nations people came to listen to Solomon's wisdom . . ." 1 Kings 4:29-34

Red squirrels always a joy to watch.

Top: Chaffinch   *Top right*: Great Spotted Woodpecker.

Right: Great Tit

Left clockwise: Pine Marten (a thrill to see a pine marten!),

Eurasian Jays squawking, Cock Pheasant, Female Pheasant

So lovely to be out and about.

Glen Isla Angus

It is peaceful by the river but after a while, just as we are beginning to shift uncomfortably, suddenly one by one the beavers appear. One comes along with a large branch full of leaves and dives down with it to fix to the river bed. The green leaves will now be kept fresh and will provide food, even should river freeze over (unlikely). On this river they don't seem to need to build a dam but elsewhere we saw the dams, trees felled and great teeth marks on tree trunks.

September 2020

"I lift up my eyes to the mountains — where does my help come from?
My help comes from the Lord, the Maker of heaven and earth."

Psalm 121:1-2

Looking towards Glenshee

Parish church Glenshee

Left: Red Grouse – found in heather moorland in Great Britain and Ireland. They have feathered feet and toes to cope with the cold!

Bottom: Red Grouse in Glenshee taken just before Lockdown in March 2020.

Looking down Glenshee.

October 2020

"For every beast of the forest is mine, the cattle on a thousand hills. I know all the birds of the hills, and all that moves in the field is mine." Psalm 50:10-11 ESV

The squirrels quickly find the nuts in the little model supermarket trolley! They have an acute sense of smell, even detecting if a nut is rotten inside the shell and can locate them even under the snow. Buried nuts are found by a combination of memory and smell. They can also assess the weight of a nut inside its shell by handling it. Though we can only focus on a single (central) area at a time, the periphery remaining blurred, a squirrel can clearly see what's next to it and above it without moving its head. Their hearing, too, has a far greater range than ours. Red squirrels, as opposed to grey ones, have ear tufts showing most prominently in winter. and have double jointed ankles allowing them to go down tree trunks head first. The grey squirrel's memory is better though!

Left: Eurasian Jay. The male jay has been shown to feed the female with food preferable to her!

Loch Earn Perthshire

Hill pony

November 2020

"... but a mist went up from the earth and watered the whole face of the ground."
Genesis 2:6 NKJV

Roe deer run into the November mist.

The robin keeps appearing in front of me when I am trying to photograph a wren on the wood pile. He seems to want the attention (as they do). I am happy to give it.

Wren

Great Tit

December 2020

"He spreads the snow like wool and scatters the frost like ashes."
Psalm 147:16

Stonechat (their call sounds like two stones
knocking together)

Reed Bunting

Roe deer with distinctive white moustache and neck markings often come to the field nearby.

Right: Buzzard

Above: Bullfinch

Left: Cock Pheasant resting in the morning sunshine.

Right: Long Tailed Tits; such endearing little birds but scarcely seem to stay still a moment. Although I did photograph long tailed tits the same day as the pheasant on the left, they weren't as good as the ones on the right taken later.

The crows weren't far away from the buzzard on the left. The buzzard is seen as a potential threat to the crow, its young and its territory. Crows will often mob a buzzard though seldom physically attack. Likewise the buzzard rarely fights but avoids attack by skilful flying. It is to none of the birds' advantage to be hurt. Buzzards eat small mammals, birds, insects and earthworms.

Bullfinches mainly eat seeds and buds of fruit trees, so can be a bit of a nuisance to fruit growers.

January 2021

"As the rain and the snow come down from heaven, and do not return to it without watering the earth and making it bud and flourish, so that it yields seed for the sower and bread for the eater, so is my word that goes out from my mouth: it will not return to me empty, but will accomplish what I desire and achieve the purpose for which I sent it."

Isaiah 55:10-11

Left: Jay   *Top*: Blue tit   *Top right*: Yellowhammer

Second wave of Coronavirus. The new rules mean once again having to stay at home, only going out locally for exercise, essential shopping or medical reasons. Snow arrives, the birds are hungry.

The birds soon gather looking for food. It is lovely to see them — blackbirds, sparrows, blue tits, coal tits, great tits, goldfinches, chaffinches and, of course the robin.

Top left: Chaffinches   *Top right:* Goldfinch

Right clockwise: Robin having a bath the minute I had broken the ice, goldfinch, robin, chaffinch and great tit on the feeder.

A walk down the lane at the end of the road.

Top: Red Squirrel. *Top right*: Female Chaffinch looking rather sweet.

Right: Treecreeper – so quick and well camouflaged that they are difficult to spot or photograph. They go up or along the trunk or branch of a tree looking for insects but never go down. They will fly down but can't go head first down the trunk.

Far right: Tranquil evening at the estuary of the Tay.

February 2021

"And the God of all grace, who called you to his eternal glory in Christ, after you have suffered a little while, will himself restore you and make you strong, firm and steadfast." 1 Peter 5:10

What a delight to see snowdrops and crocuses appear in gardens and woods; signs of hope that Spring perhaps is not too far away. All winter the bulbs have lain in the ground with no sign of life, but the life has been there, leaves and flowers being formed in the darkness, the cold essential — till now they have broken through in all their loveliness, delicate looking but strong. Sometimes it is like that for us. That hard period of cold and dark is what allows flowers to grow and flourish, bringing hope and blessing to others.

Left: Pussy Willow Catkins

And now it snows some more, but all these beauties come to cheer. What colours, what design!

Left: Male Chaffinch and Blue tit.   *Top*: Goldfinch and Robin

Another walk down the lane at the end of the road. Red squirrel with dirty nose and snow on his whiskers! A stonechat pauses on some weeds.

The countryside is transformed by the snowfall — a delight for a little while!

March 2021

"The God who made the world and everything in it .... he himself gives everyone life and breath and everything else."   Acts 17:24-25

Male Siskin looking smart

  Checking he's looking his best!

Left: The time for singing has come again!
Robin giving it all he has.

Left: Robin drinking   *Above*: Male Siskin

Unexpected visit from
female woodpecker and
first ever redpoll (above).
The redpoll visited
another couple of times,
but hasn't been back that I
have noticed.

And so a year passes. Spring comes, only seeming to vanish again as snow and ice suddenly reappear. Finally, almost reluctantly, days get a little warmer, blossoms blossom and new young wildlife appear. Ospreys arrive from Africa and build their great nest. The rhythm of life goes on. What amazing life it is; most of us understanding little of the layer upon layer of complex workings involved in each individual part – but it has been a delight to observe.

Finally restrictions here are lifting; once again friends can come into our homes! What a joy.

While for some, like myself, this past year has brought new opportunities and blessings, for many it has been really hard in a whole variety of ways. Death has come very close, whether to the one facing it imminently, to those who have lost loved ones, to the ones on the front line fighting for people's lives or just simply the reminders of death brought by listening to the news. The question must surely have been in many minds, "What happens when we die?" We tend not to talk about it much but it is a question that needs to be faced and settled in our minds. We have all done wrong – but for the one who believes and embraces that when Jesus Christ came to this earth, it was to suffer and die for our sin, for that person comes forgiveness and the assurance that death is only the door to a new life more wonderful than can be imagined. Read what Jesus himself said, (search for "John 3:14-21" – "lifted up" means on the Cross.)

As millions can testify, we can have, not a 'religion' but a relationship with Him now and eternally, a relationship which brings with it a sure knowledge that He is there, bringing peace and help through all the difficulties of life. Through our experiences with Him now, we know we can trust His word for the future. If there is so much beauty and variety in the natural world, think what it will be in the next eternal world!

"He will wipe every tear from their eyes. There will be no more death or mourning or crying or pain, for the old order of things has passed away."   Revelation 21:4